St. Helena Library

# The Seminole

## by Petra Press

Content Adviser: Professor Sherry L. Field,
Department of Social Science Education, College of Education,
The University of Georgia

Reading Adviser: Dr. Linda D. Labbo,
Department of Reading Education, College of Education,
The University of Georgia

 **COMPASS POINT BOOKS**

Minneapolis, Minnesota

Compass Point Books
3722 West 50th Street, #115
Minneapolis, MN 55410

Visit Compass Point Books on the Internet at *www.compasspointbooks.com* or e-mail your request
to *custserv@compasspointbooks.com*

Front cover: A Seminole shoulder bag from 1825

Photographs ©: The Detroit Institute of Arts (Shoulder bag, c. 1825, Seminole, Founders Society
Purchase, 1992), cover; Graeme Teague, 4, 19, 37, 41; Hulton Getty/Archive Photos, 5, 16, 24, 34;
North Wind Picture Archives, 7, 9, 11, 21, 23, 28; XNR Productions, Inc., 8; Marilyn "Angel"
Wynn, 12, 13, 14, 25, 30, 36, 39, 40, 42, 43; Archive Photos, 15, 20, 32; Max and Bea Hunn/
Visuals Unlimited, 17, 27; Unicorn Stock Photos/Jim Shippee, 18; Stock Montage, 22; The
Newberry Library/Stock Montage, 26; Willie Hill/FPG International, 29; William J. Weber/Visuals
Unlimited, 31; Lake County Museum/Corbis, 33; Denver Public Library, Western History
Collection, 34; Peter Turnley/Corbis, 35.

Editors: E. Russell Primm, Emily J. Dolbear, and Alice K. Flanagan
Photo Researcher: Svetlana Zhurkina
Photo Selector: Catherine Neitge
Designer: Bradfordesign, Inc.

**Library of Congress Cataloging-in-Publication Data**
Press, Petra.
   The Seminole / by Petra Press.
      p. cm. — (First reports)
   Includes bibliographical references and index.
   ISBN 0-7565-0083-4 (hardcover : lib. bldg.)
   1. Seminole Indians—History—Juvenile literature. 2. Seminole Indians—Social life and cus-
toms—Juvenile literature. 3. Seminole Indians—Government relations—Juvenile literature. [1.
Seminole Indians. 2. Indians of North America—Southern States.] I. Title. II. Series.
E99.S28 P74 2001
975.9'004973—dc21                                                                    00-011283

# Table of Contents

▲ A young Seminole boy dances at a festival in south Florida.

# Who Are the Seminole?

Long ago, the Seminole (pronounced SEM-uh-nole) belonged to many different Native American tribes. The tribes lived in the southern United States. They lived in what are now the states of Florida, Georgia, and Alabama.

▲ *A Seminole village in the southern United States*

Over many years, the tribes banded together in Florida. Later, runaway black slaves joined them. These groups became a nation of people called the Seminole.

In the 1500s, explorers from Europe began to arrive in the Americas. The Spaniards came to Florida in 1513.

The Spanish explorers found four Native American tribes living in Florida. The Calusa (kuh-LOO-suh) were on the west coast. The Timucua (tih-MOO-koo-uh) and Tekesta (tu-KESS-tuh) were on the east coast. The Apalachee (ap-uh-LAY-chee) were in the north.

# The Spanish and the British

Before long, the Spaniards built large camps called forts along the Florida coast. They took control of Florida.

▲ *Spanish soldiers came to Florida in the 1500s.*

Legend:
- Present-day Seminole reservations
- Battle site

Kansas

Missouri

Illinois

Indiana

Ohio

Kentucky

CHEROKEE

Arkansas

Oklahoma

CREEK
SEMINOLE
CHOCTAW

Arkansas

Tennessee

North Carolina

CHEROKEE

South Carolina

CREEK

Texas

Louisiana

CHOCTAW

Mississippi

Alabama

Georgia

First Seminole
War, 1816–1818

ATLANTIC
OCEAN

SEMINOLE

Second Seminole
War, 1835–1842

Florida

Gulf of Mexico

SEMINOLE

Third Seminole
War, 1855–1858

N
W E
S

0          150 miles
0          150 kilometers

▲ A map of past and present Seminole lands

Then people from Britain came. They attacked the Spanish forts. Then they took the land. By the 1700s, British settlers had moved into Alabama and Georgia.

The British did not get along with the Indians who

▲ *Many Creek Indians moved to Florida.*

lived in the area. The Indians living there were Creek. Many Creek families ran away to northern Florida. They wanted to get away from the British.

The Creek called the Indians who ran away the "Seminole." *Seminole* is a Creek word meaning "runaway."

In time, the British **colonies** grew larger. People who lived in colonies were called colonists. They were farmers who grew cotton and tobacco. The British colonists bought slaves from Africa to work in their fields.

In 1775, the colonists went to war against Britain. They wanted to be free of Britain. They wanted their own government.

In 1783, the colonists won. They set up a new country called the United States of America.

Over the years, some African slaves who worked in the colonies escaped to Florida. They joined the Creek and other Indian tribes there.

# Life in Northern Florida

When the Seminole first came to Florida, they lived in the north. They lived much like their Creek relatives.

The women grew corn, beans, and squash. The men raised cattle and horses. They hunted deer, bear, and rabbits. They caught fish in traps called **weirs**.

▲ *Seminole hunters used spears and a wooden trap called a weir to catch fish.*

The Seminole made canoes out of tree bark. They also carved **dugouts** from cypress logs. Some canoes were 40 to 50 feet (12 to 15 meters) long.

The Seminole traveled far in their canoes. Some Seminole explorers may have gone as far south as Cuba and the Bahamas.

▲ *A canoe carved from a cypress tree*

▲ *Seminole women make colorful dolls.*

The Seminole were good with their hands. The women wove baskets and made pottery. They made Indian dolls. The men carved wood into tools, weapons, and pipes. They also made beautiful silver jewelry.

Today, visitors to Florida buy Seminole baskets woven out of pine needles and sweet grass. The colorful Seminole dolls are popular too.

▲ *Seminole baskets for sale*

# Clans and Villages

▲ *Two Seminole men in a cypress canoe*

The Florida Seminole lived in large villages near the Spanish settlements. The two groups often traded with each other.

Over time, the Seminole learned Spanish ways. They hunted with guns. They cooked with iron pots, kettles, and knives. Rich Seminole farmers lived in large, beautiful houses. Some even rode in carriages pulled by horses.

In the center of every Seminole town was a town square. A meetinghouse and other community buildings stood in the square. Twenty to thirty houses stood around the meetinghouse. Sometimes, large fences surrounded the towns.

A **tribal council** met in the meetinghouse. The tribal council was a group of Seminole leaders. They chose war chiefs. They also passed laws.

Creek and Seminole traditions were a lot like

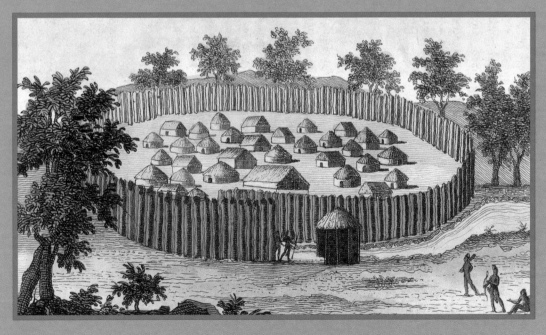

▲ *A Florida Seminole village surrounded by a fence*

European traditions. The settlers called these Indians "civilized." They were two of the "Five Civilized Tribes" of the Southeast. The other three were the Choctaw, Cherokee, and Chickasaw.

Seminole families lived in groups called **clans**. Some clan names were Panther, Bear, Wind, Bird, Snake, and Otter. Today, the largest is the Panther Clan.

Seminole women were the heads of the house. Children were born into their mother's clan. When children married, a son went to live with his wife's family. They lived with the wife's family for a few years. Then they started a new camp.

▲ *Seminole women were heads of the family.*

# Seminole Religion

▲ *A medicine man*

The Seminole believed that spirits lived in all things. They believed that spirits lived in animals, rocks, rivers, and trees. So they respected every natural thing.

The Seminole held **ceremonies** to show their respect for the spirits. A priest or medicine man led the ceremonies.

The most important Seminole ceremony was the Green Corn Dance. They held it every year when the corn was ripe. It marked the start of a new year.

▲ *Seminole dancers take part in a festival.*

Many things happened during the Green Corn Dance. Sick people were healed. Men and women were married or divorced. They carried out tribal business. Children learned their religious duties.

It was also a time for eating, dancing, and playing games. Today the Green Corn Dance is still an important Seminole tradition.

# The Seminole Wars

In the 1800s, American settlers built homes and farmed on Seminole land in Florida. By now, the land belonged to Spain.

The Seminole and the settlers fought often over land. They also fought over African slaves. Runaway slaves from Georgia and Alabama lived with the Seminole. American **plantation** owners often attacked Seminole towns in search of slaves.

◄ A Seminole chief named Tuko-see Mathla

In 1817, the United States began a war with the Seminole in Florida. It was called the First Seminole War. U.S. general Andrew Jackson and his troops burned down Seminole villages.

Spain did not protect Florida. Instead, Spain sold Florida to the United States.

▲ *The First Seminole War began in 1817.*

The settlers wanted the Seminole to leave northern Florida. In 1823, the Seminole signed a **treaty** with the United States. They gave up most of their land. They moved to a **reservation** in the center of Florida.

In return, the U.S. government promised to give Indians money, farming tools, and cattle. It also promised to protect them from more settlers.

▲ *General Andrew Jackson and his troops in Florida in the First Seminole War*

▲ *U.S. troops captured Seminole chiefs during the First Seminole War.*

But the land on the reservation was bad for farming and hunting. Before long, people were starving.

Then in 1830, the U.S government passed a law. This law forced the Seminole and other Native Americans to move to Indian Territory. It was land in what is now the state of Oklahoma.

▲ *Soldiers hunted the Indians with bloodhounds during the Second Seminole War.*

Most Seminole would not leave their land. This started the Second Seminole War in 1835. For seven years, the Seminole fought U.S. soldiers.

Osceola and Coacoochee (Wildcat) were two brave Seminole chiefs. They led the Seminole in their fight. Both men were captured. Osceola died in prison. Wildcat escaped. He fought for four more years. Then he was moved to Oklahoma.

By 1841, most Seminole agreed to move west. Others traveled south into swamps called the Florida Everglades. Swamps are lands almost entirely covered with water. The Seminole believed the soldiers would not follow them there.

▲ *Chief Osceola on a hunting trip*

▲ *Chief Bolek (Billy Bowlegs)*

Then in 1855, the Third Seminole War began. Chief Bolek (Billy Bowlegs) led the Seminole against the Americans. This war lasted for three years. That was the last time the Seminole fought U.S. soldiers.

In 1858, about 250 more Seminole Indians were sent to Oklahoma. The rest never gave up. Their relatives live in Florida today.

# People of the Everglades

The weather was wet and hot in the Everglades. The Seminole learned new ways there.

They built special houses from palm trees. The houses had roofs of palm leaves. They were open on all fours sides to let breezes in. These houses were called **chickees**.

▲ *Seminole chickees are open on all sides.*

▲ *A Seminole village in the Everglades*

The Seminole sometimes built chickees about 3 feet (91 centimeters) off the ground. That kept out mud and water.

Each family had three chickees. They cooked and ate their meals in one chickee. They slept in the second chickee. And they relaxed and told stories in the third.

The Seminole built chickees on clumps of higher

ground called **hammocks**. Hammocks were the only dry land in the swamp.

The Seminole cleared land for gardens. The women planted corn, sweet potatoes, pumpkins, sugarcane, and beans there.

▲ *A Seminole woman in traditional clothing*

The men provided the meat. They hunted turkey, ducks, rabbits, squirrels, alligators, otters, and birds.

The Seminoles' buckskin clothing was too warm for the Everglades. So they made new clothes. They used cloth from traders. Their clothes protected them from insects.

Women wore long skirts with capelike blouses. Men wore shirts that went down to their knees. They also wore hats with feathers.

▲ *Seminole men wearing long shirts and hats with feathers*

# Reservation Life

▲ *A Seminole homesite in the Everglades*

Life was hard on the reservations. From the 1870s to the 1920s, it was hard to find work. The people always needed more food. Many people died of disease. The children did not have good schools. Most Seminole had to give up their ways and ceremonies.

During the 1890s, the U.S. government sent Indian children to special schools. They taught the children to dress and speak like American children there. They were not allowed to speak their own language. Children lived apart from their families for many years.

But in 1934, the U.S. Congress passed a law that improved life on the reservations. This law helped

▲ *Teacher and students at an Indian school in Florida in the late 1800s*

▲ *Seminole children in 1928*

Native Americans set up tribal governments and businesses. It also helped them find their Indian arts and traditions again.

# The Oklahoma Seminole

Today, most Seminole live on reservations in Florida and Oklahoma. More than 6,000 Seminole live in Oklahoma.

The Seminole Tribe of Oklahoma has fourteen bands or groups. Two of the bands are called Freedmen Bands. They are related to the slaves who lived with the Seminole in the 1800s.

▲ *A Seminole man and woman in about 1910*

▲ *At a Seminole festival in Oklahoma City, Oklahoma*

The Oklahoma Seminole live and work like other Americans. They live in modern houses and their children go to public schools.

Some Seminole are doctors, lawyers, computer programmers, and teachers. Some are cattle ranchers or fruit growers. Others are artists, writers, or musicians. Today, only a few Seminole in Oklahoma continue to speak their own language.

# The Florida Seminole

▲ Children play on the Big Cypress Reservation.

About 3,000 Seminole live in Florida. There are two groups of Seminole in Florida. They are the Miccosukee (mih-KOS-oo-kee) and the Muskogee (mus-KOH-gee).

The Florida Seminole have six reservations. The Big Cypress Reservation in the southern Everglades is the largest. The Fort Pierce Reservation is the smallest. It was created in 1995. The Seminole Tribe of Florida headquarters is in Hollywood, Florida.

▲ *Tribal headquarters in Hollywood, Florida*

In 1962, the U.S. government gave the Everglades to the Florida Seminole. Today, some Seminole guide hunters and fishers in the Everglades. A few Seminole still hunt and fish on their own. But they do it mostly for sport.

Some Florida Seminole farm and raise cattle on the reservation. Others make their living selling their beautiful arts and crafts.

◄ *A Seminole man hunts for frogs in a dugout canoe.*

▲ A Seminole girl in traditional dress

▲ Billy L. Cypress is executive director of the Ah-Tah-Thi-Ki Museum.

The Florida Seminole earn money from visitors. The Big Cypress Reservation has campgrounds, places to hunt, and a wildlife park. The Ah-Tah-Thi-Ki Museum on the reservation has an old Seminole village. The Tampa, Brighton, Immokalee, and Hollywood Reservations have clubs and casinos. Visitors to south Florida can even watch alligator wrestling.

▲ *Alligator wrestling in south Florida is a Seminole tradition.*

▲ *People like to collect bows and arrows used for hunting.*

▲ *The Seminole use canoes and airboats in the Everglades.*

In the past, the Seminole fought bravely for their land and their freedom. Then, they learned to live in a new land. Today, Seminole Americans live bravely in two worlds—one traditional and one modern.

# Glossary

**ceremonies**—formal actions to mark important times

**chickees**—houses made of palm trees and open on four sides

**clans**—groups of related families

**colonies**—groups of people who live in newly settled areas

**dugouts**—canoes made by digging out the inside of a log

**hammocks**—dry land in the swamp

**plantation**—a large farm with crops such as cotton or tobacco

**reservation**—a large area of land set aside for Native Americans; in Canada reservations are called reserves

**treaty**—an agreement between two governments

**tribal council**—a group of people chosen to make important decisions for a tribe

**weirs**—wooden traps set in the water to catch fish

## Did You Know?

- Chief Osceola was one of the most brilliant military leaders of the 1800s.

- Florida's state capital—Tallahassee—got its name from a Muskogee word meaning "old town."

- About 1,500 U.S. soldiers died in the Seminole wars.

- The U.S. government spent more than $30 million fighting the Seminole.

## At a Glance

**Tribal name:** Seminole

**Past locations:** Florida, Georgia, Alabama

**Present locations:** Florida, Oklahoma

**Traditional houses:** Houses made of palm trees and open on four sides called chickees

**Traditional clothing materials:** Skins; later, colorful cloth and feathers

**Traditional transportation:** Dugout canoes

**Traditional food:** Corn, beans, squash, fish, small game, wild plants

# Important Dates

| | |
|---|---|
| **1500s** | European explorers come to the Americas. Spaniards take the land that is now Florida in 1513. |
| **1700s** | British settlers move into Alabama and Georgia. Creek Indians leave to settle in northern Florida. |
| **1817–1818** | The United States and the Seminole fight in the First Seminole War. Spain sells Florida land to the United States. |
| **1823** | The Seminole give up their land and move to a reservation in the center of Florida. |
| **1830** | The U.S government forces the Seminole to move to Indian Territory. |
| **1835–1842** | The Second Seminole War takes place. |
| **1838** | Chief Osceola dies in prison. |
| **1855–1858** | The Third Seminole War takes place. |
| **1962** | U.S. government gives the Florida Everglades to the Seminole. |
| **1970** | The Indian Claims Commission pays the Seminole $12,347,500 for the land that was taken from them in Oklahoma. |

# Want to Know More?

## At the Library
Brooks, Barbara. *The Seminole*. Vero Beach, Fla.: Rourke
Publications, Inc., 1989.
Koslow, Philip. *The Seminole Indians*. New York: Chelsea Juniors,
1994.
Sneve, Virginia Driving Hawk. *The Seminoles*. New York: Holiday
House, 1994.

## On the Web
### The Seminole Tribe of Florida
*http://www.seminoletribe.com*
For information on the history and culture of the Florida Seminole

### Seminole Nation of Oklahoma
*http://www.cowboy.net/native/seminole/index.html*
For information on the history and culture of the Oklahoma
Seminole

## Through the Mail
### The Seminole Tribe of Florida
6300 Stirling Road
Hollywood, FL 33024
To get more information about the Seminole Tribe of Florida

## On the Road
### Ah-Tah-Thi-Ki Museum
On Big Cypress Seminole Reservation
Clewiston, FL 33440
800/949-6101
To see exhibits on the history and culture of the Seminole, a
Seminole village, and boardwalk nature trails

# Index

## About the Author

Petra Press is a freelance writer of young adult nonfiction, specializing in the diverse culture of the Americas. Her more than twenty books include histories of U.S. immigration, education, and settlement of the West, as well as portraits of numerous indigenous cultures. She lives with her husband, David, in Milwaukee, Wisconsin.